# THE ARIZONA CARDINALS

BY JANIE SCHEFFER

EPIC

BELLWETHER MEDIA ★ MINNEAPOLIS, MN

# EPIC

**EPIC BOOKS** are no ordinary books. They burst with intense action, high-speed heroics, and shadows of the unknown. Are you ready for an Epic adventure?

This book is intended for educational use. Organization and franchise logos are trademarks of the National Football League (NFL). This is not an official book of the NFL. It is not approved by or connected with the NFL.

This edition first published in 2024 by Bellwether Media, Inc.

No part of this publication may be reproduced in whole or in part without written permission of the publisher. For information regarding permission, write to Bellwether Media, Inc., Attention: Permissions Department, 6012 Blue Circle Drive, Minnetonka, MN 55343.

Library of Congress Cataloging-in-Publication Data

Names: Scheffer, Janie, 1992- author.
Title: The Arizona Cardinals / by Janie Scheffer.
Description: Minneapolis, MN : Bellwether Media, 2024. | Series: Epic. NFL team profiles | Includes bibliographical references and index. | Audience: Ages 7-12 | Audience: Grades 2-3 | Summary: "Engaging images accompany information about the Arizona Cardinals. The combination of high-interest subject matter and light text is intended for students in grades 2 through 7"-- Provided by publisher.
Identifiers: LCCN 2023021281 (print) | LCCN 2023021282 (ebook) | ISBN 9798886874662 (library binding) | ISBN 9798886876543 (ebook)
Subjects: LCSH: Arizona Cardinals (Football team)--History--Juvenile literature. | St. Louis Cardinals (Football team)--History--Juvenile literature.
Classification: LCC GV956.A75 S35 2024 (print) | LCC GV956.A75 (ebook) | DDC 796.332/640979173--dc23/eng/20230518
LC record available at https://lccn.loc.gov/2023021281
LC ebook record available at https://lccn.loc.gov/2023021282

Text copyright © 2024 by Bellwether Media, Inc. EPIC and associated logos are trademarks and/or registered trademarks of Bellwether Media, Inc.

Editor: Kieran Downs    Designer: Josh Brink

Printed in the United States of America, North Mankato, MN.

# TABLE OF CONTENTS

| | |
|---|---|
| **MURRAY'S MAGICAL PLAY** | 4 |
| **THE HISTORY OF THE CARDINALS** | 6 |
| **THE CARDINALS TODAY** | 14 |
| **GAME DAY!** | 16 |
| **ARIZONA CARDINALS FACTS** | 20 |
| **GLOSSARY** | 22 |
| **TO LEARN MORE** | 23 |
| **INDEX** | 24 |

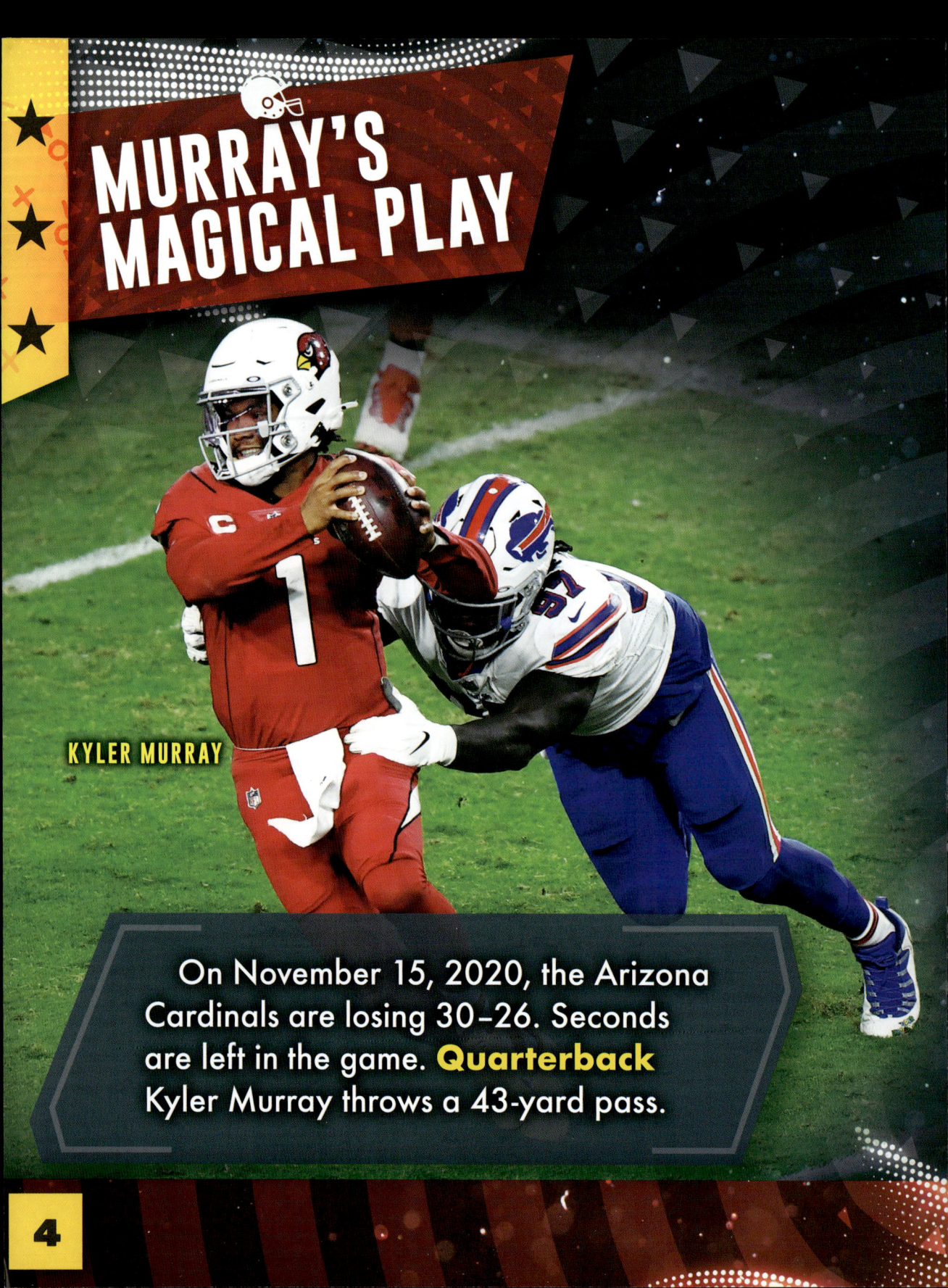

# MURRAY'S MAGICAL PLAY

KYLER MURRAY

On November 15, 2020, the Arizona Cardinals are losing 30–26. Seconds are left in the game. **Quarterback** Kyler Murray throws a 43-yard pass.

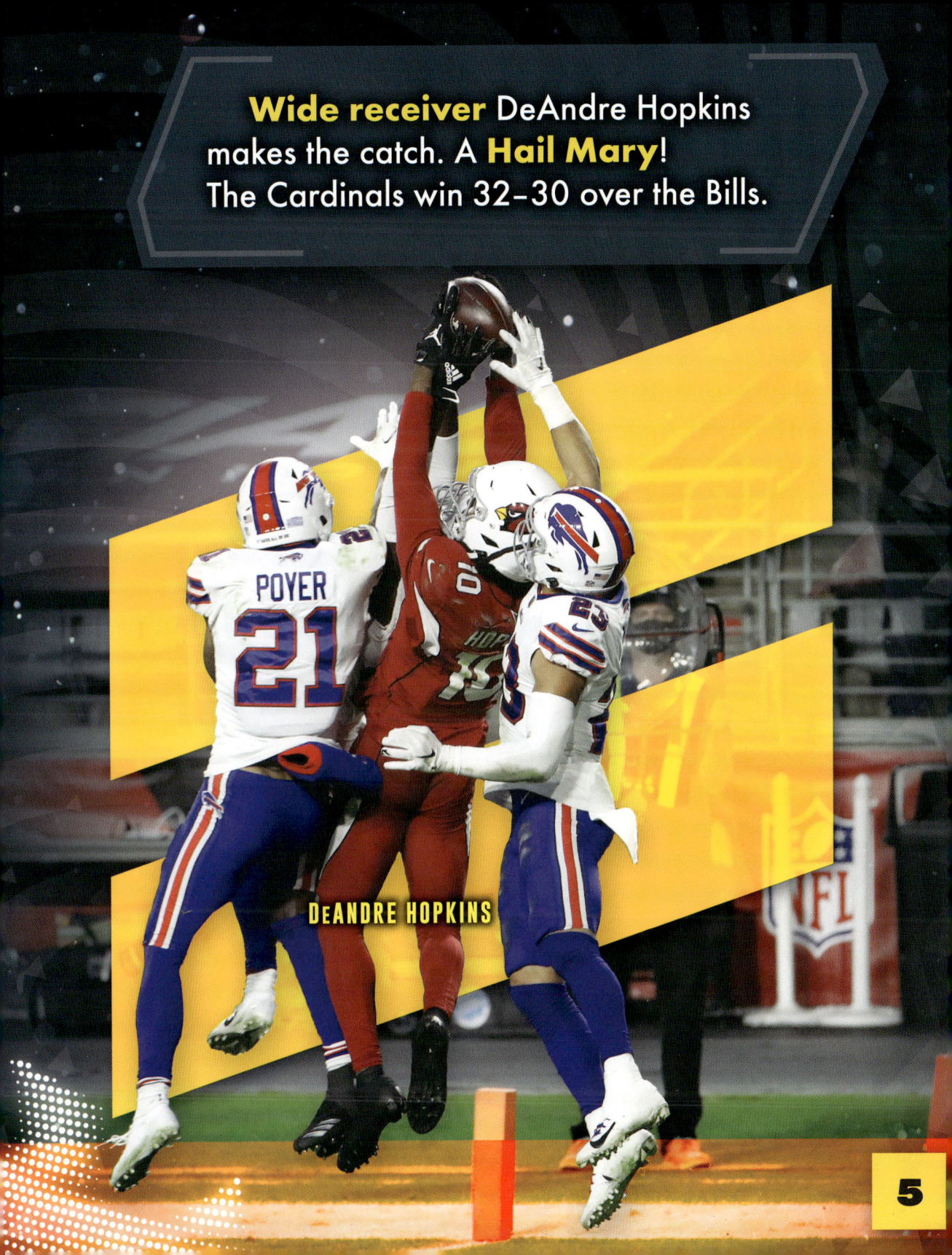

**Wide receiver** DeAndre Hopkins makes the catch. A **Hail Mary**! The Cardinals win 32–30 over the Bills.

DeAndre Hopkins

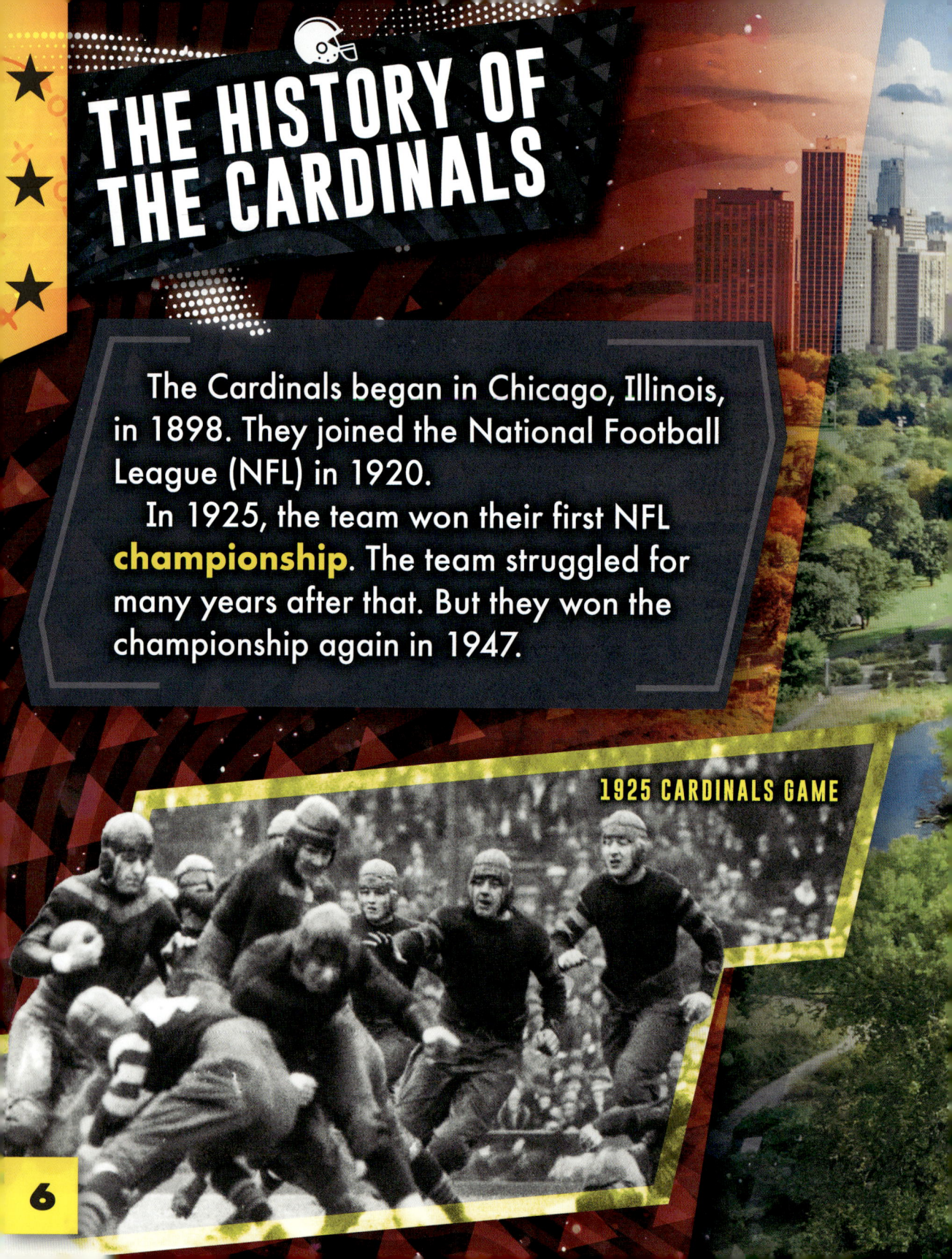

# THE HISTORY OF THE CARDINALS

The Cardinals began in Chicago, Illinois, in 1898. They joined the National Football League (NFL) in 1920.

In 1925, the team won their first NFL **championship**. The team struggled for many years after that. But they won the championship again in 1947.

**1925 CARDINALS GAME**

## OLD JERSEYS, NEW NAME

The Cardinals' name comes from the team's first owner. Chris O'Brien bought used red jerseys from the University of Chicago. He said they were cardinal red.

**CHICAGO, ILLINOIS**

JIM HART

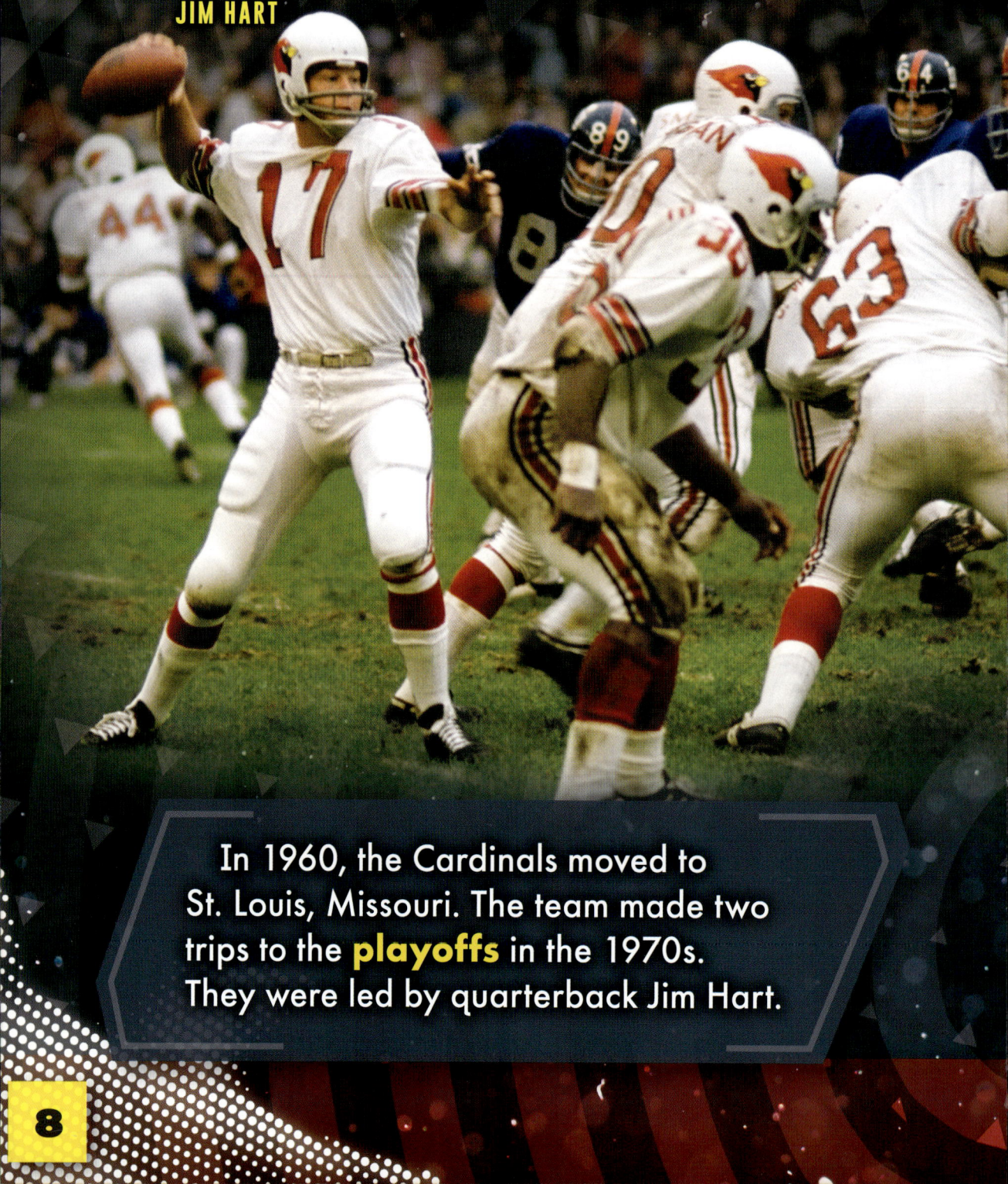

In 1960, the Cardinals moved to St. Louis, Missouri. The team made two trips to the **playoffs** in the 1970s. They were led by quarterback Jim Hart.

The Cardinals' success faded in the 1980s. In 1988, the team moved to Phoenix, Arizona.

1988 CARDINALS GAME

The Cardinals struggled again in the 1990s. In 1999, they won their first playoff game in over 50 years.

**1999 PLAYOFF GAME**

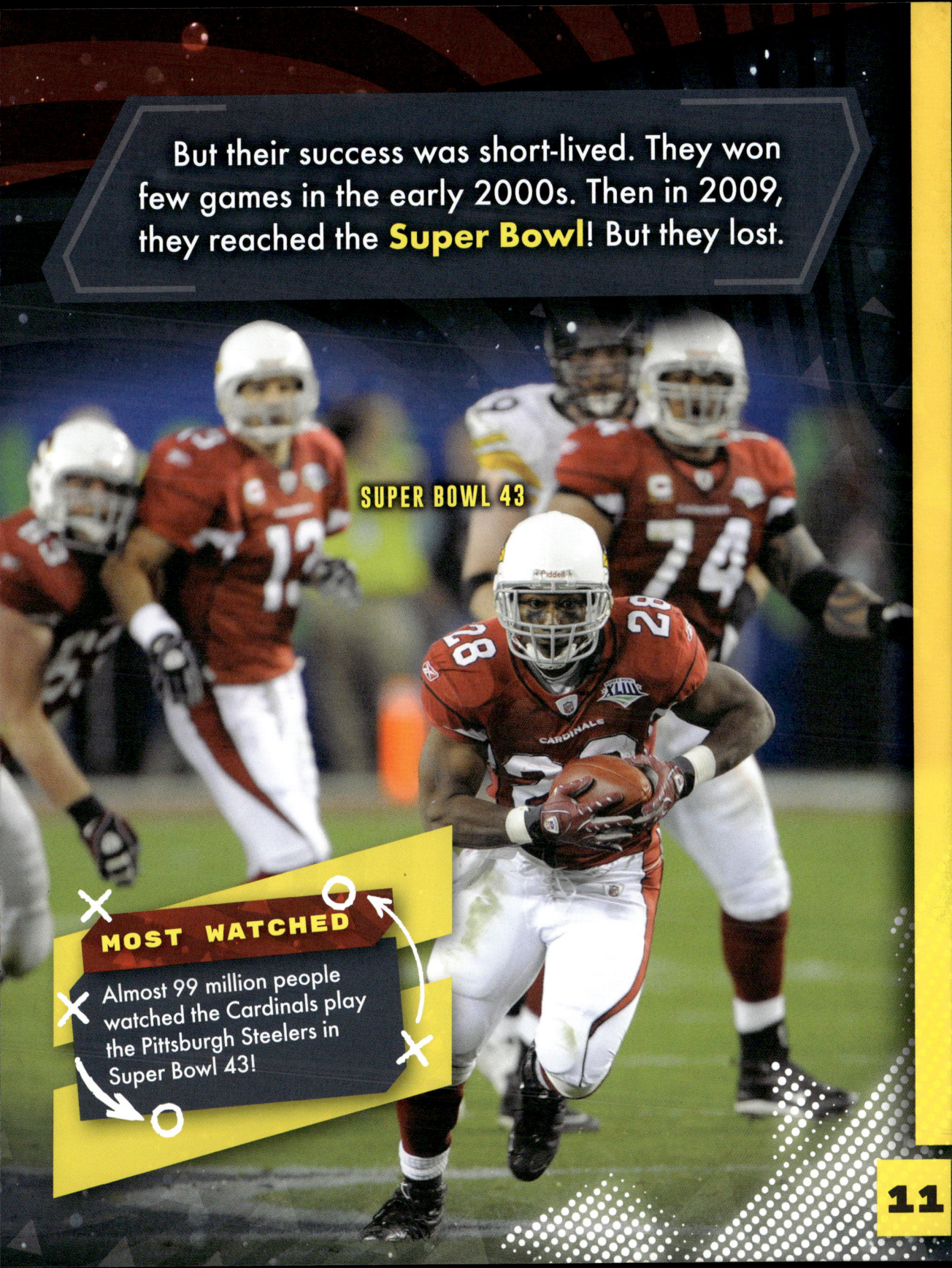

But their success was short-lived. They won few games in the early 2000s. Then in 2009, they reached the **Super Bowl**! But they lost.

SUPER BOWL 43

### MOST WATCHED

Almost 99 million people watched the Cardinals play the Pittsburgh Steelers in Super Bowl 43!

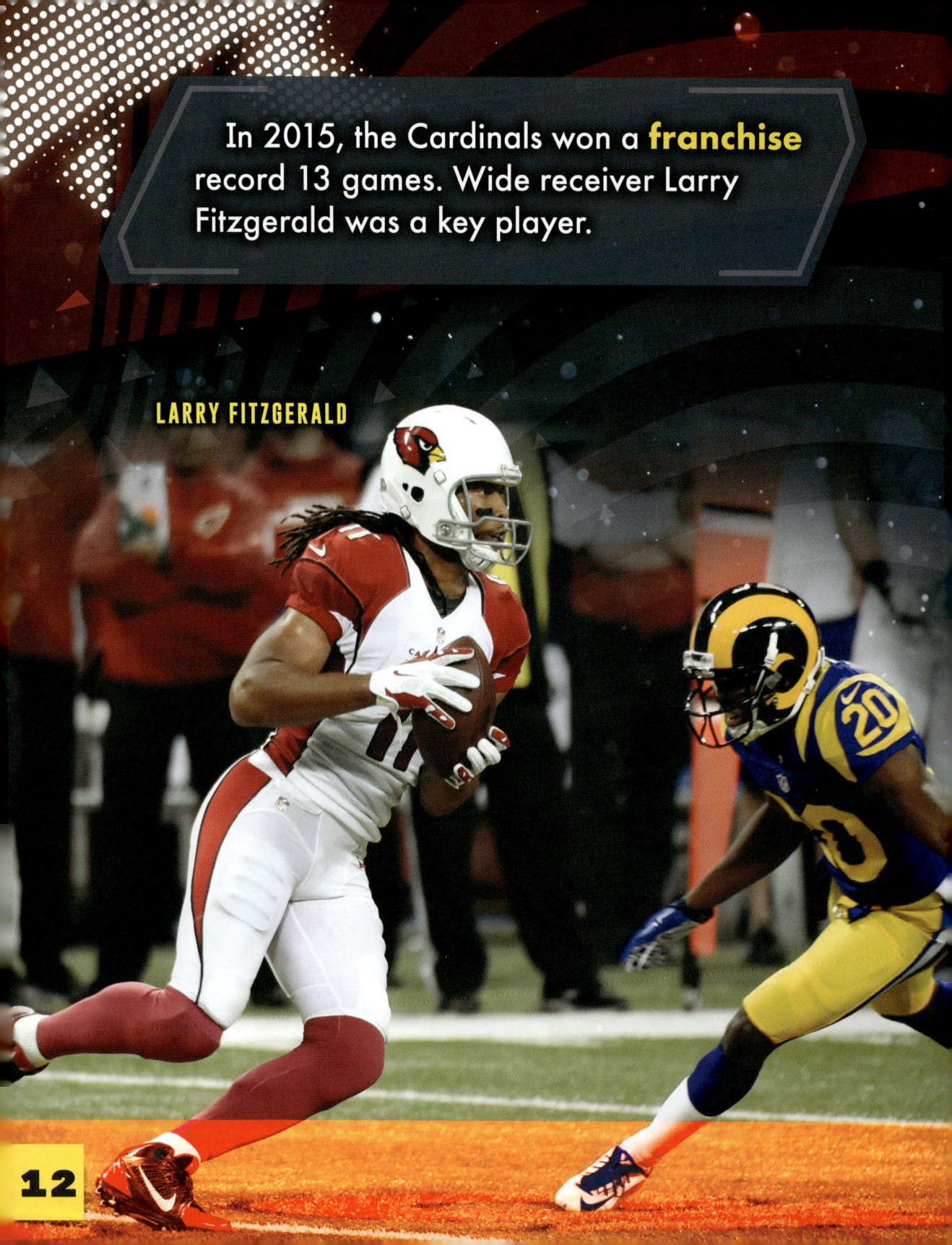

In 2015, the Cardinals won a **franchise** record 13 games. Wide receiver Larry Fitzgerald was a key player.

LARRY FITZGERALD

The Cardinals struggled in the late 2010s. But in 2021, quarterback Kyler Murray led the team back to the playoffs!

## TROPHY CASE

**NFC WEST championships**
3

**NFC championships**
1

**PLAYOFF appearances**
11

**NFL championships**
2

# THE CARDINALS TODAY

CARDINALS VS. SEAHAWKS

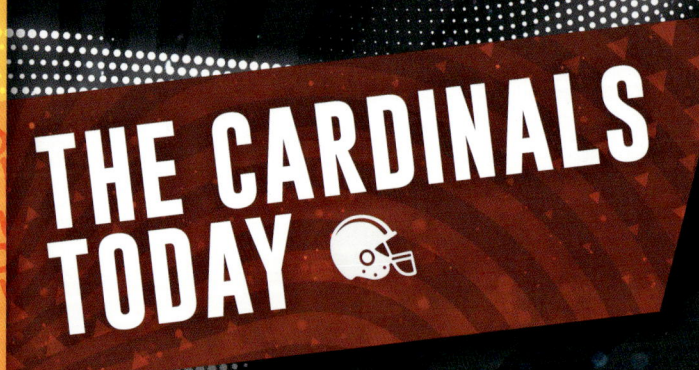

The Cardinals play in Glendale, Arizona, at State Farm **Stadium**. It has a **retractable** playing field and roof.

14

The team plays in the NFC West **division**. Their biggest **rivals** are the Seattle Seahawks and the San Francisco 49ers.

### OLD RIVALS

The Cardinals' first rival was the Chicago Bears. They first played each other over 100 years ago!

## LOCATION

ARIZONA

**STATE FARM STADIUM**

Glendale, Arizona

15

# GAME DAY!

Before home games, the Big Red Siren sounds. This pumps up the team and fans. Big Red is also the name of the team's **mascot**. He wears red and black, the team's colors.

BIG RED SIREN

BIG RED

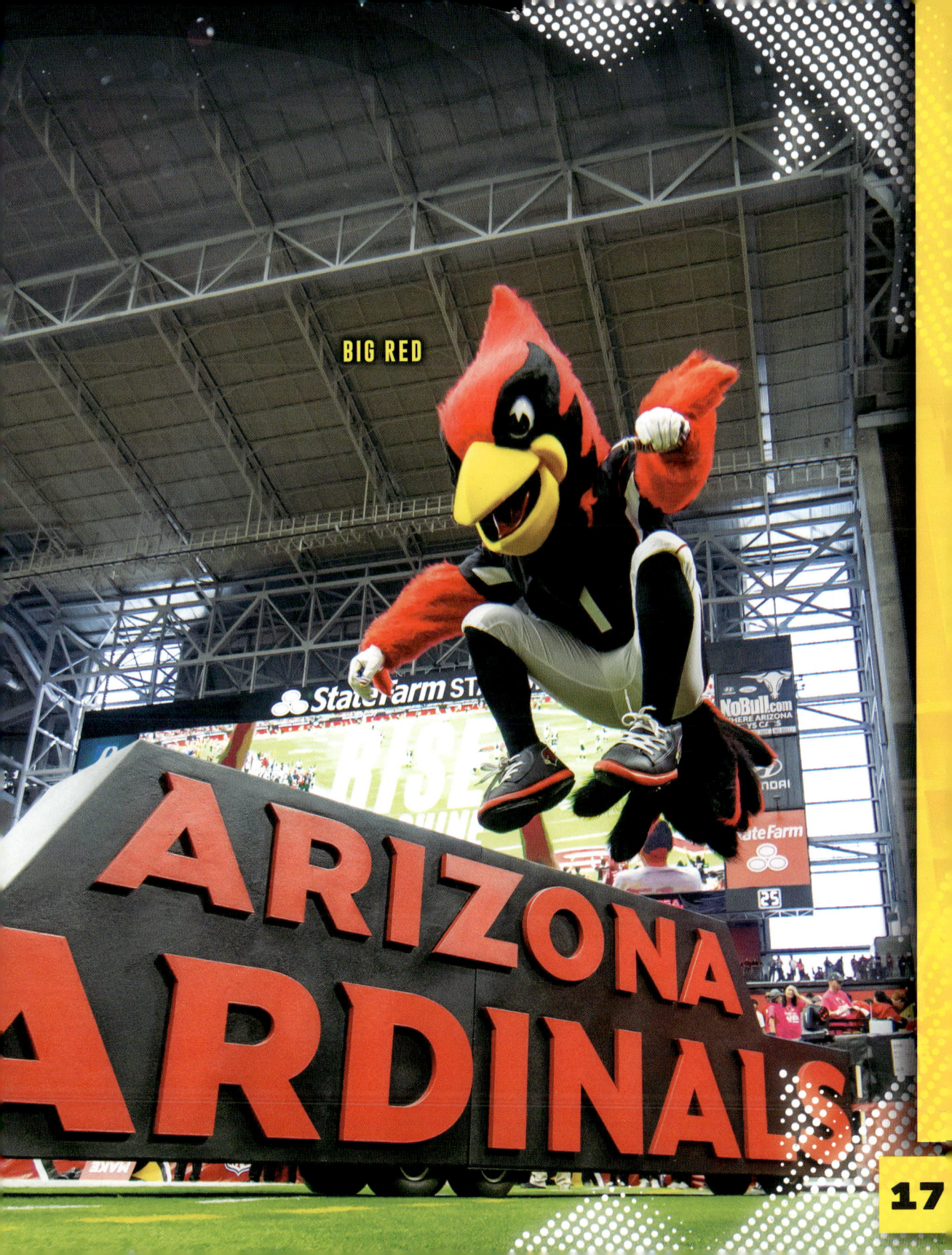

ARIZONA CARDINALS

Cardinals fans call themselves the "Bird Gang." They dress in cardinal red. They root for their team with the cheer "Rise up, Red Sea!" They are proud to support the oldest team in the NFL!

# ★ FAMOUS PLAYERS

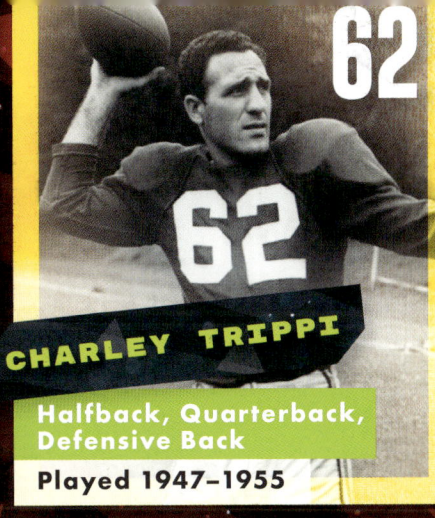

**62**

### CHARLEY TRIPPI
**Halfback, Quarterback, Defensive Back**
Played 1947–1955

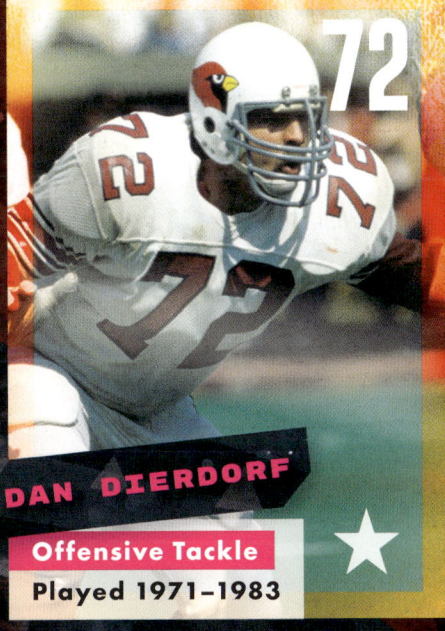

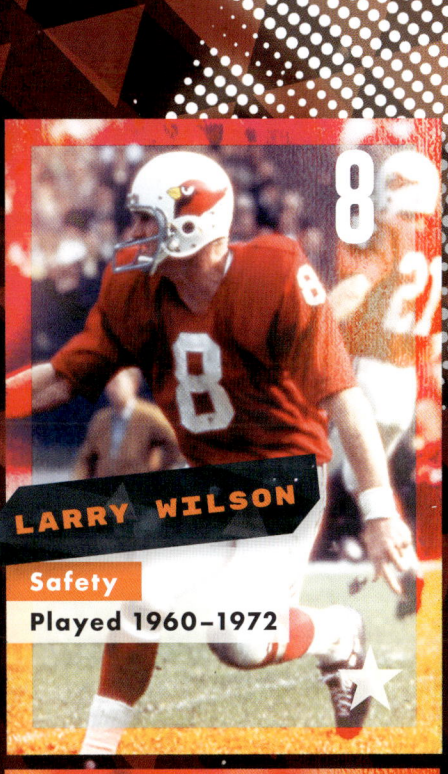

**8**

### LARRY WILSON
**Safety**
Played 1960–1972

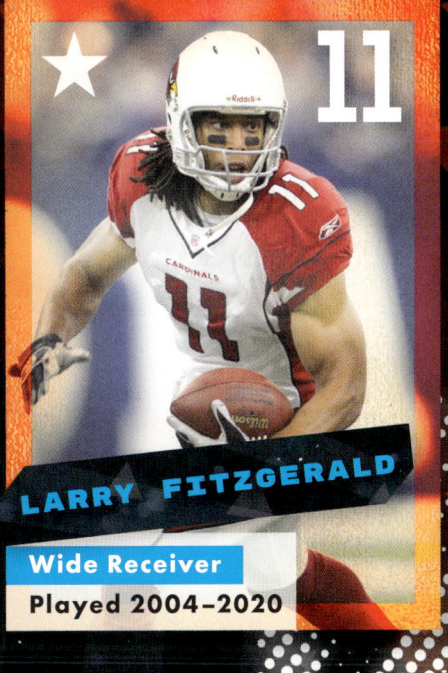

**72**

### DAN DIERDORF
**Offensive Tackle**
Played 1971–1983

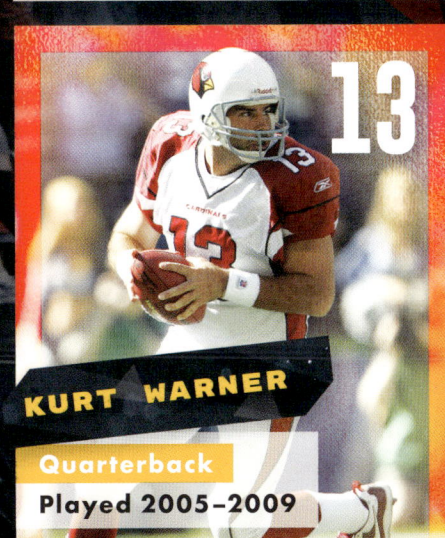

**11**

### LARRY FITZGERALD
**Wide Receiver**
Played 2004–2020

**13**

### KURT WARNER
**Quarterback**
Played 2005–2009

19

# ARIZONA CARDINALS FACTS

**LOGO**

| JOINED THE NFL | 1920 |
|---|---|
| NICKNAMES | Red Sea, The Cards |

**MASCOT: BIG RED**

**CONFERENCE**: National Football Conference (NFC)

**COLORS**

**DIVISION** | NFC West
- Los Angeles Rams
- San Francisco 49ers
- Seattle Seahawks

**STADIUM**

## STATE FARM STADIUM
opened August 1, 2006

holds 63,400 people

20

# 🕐 TIMELINE

**1898** — The Cardinals begin in Chicago

**1925** — The Cardinals win their first NFL championship

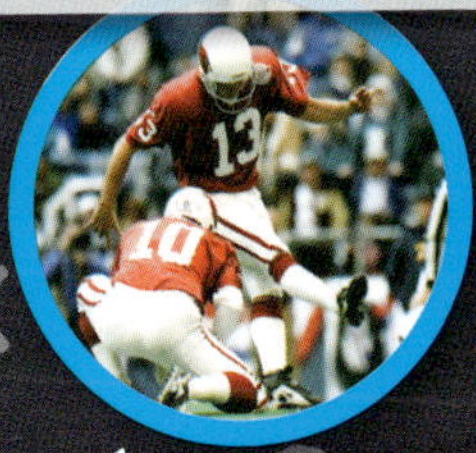

**1999** — The Cardinals win their first playoff game in over 50 years

**2009** — The Cardinals play against the Steelers in Super Bowl 43

**2015** — The Cardinals set a franchise record of 13 wins

# ★ RECORDS ★

**All-Time Passing Leader** 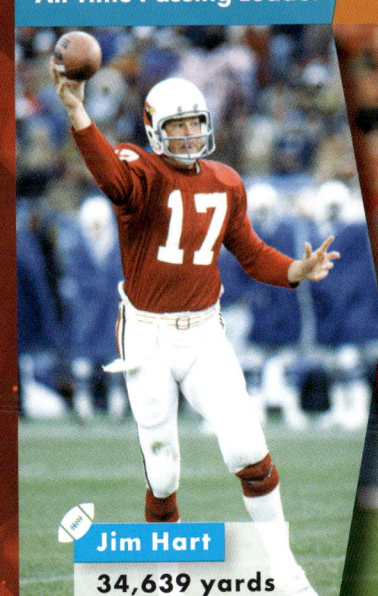
Jim Hart
34,639 yards

**All-Time Receiving Leader** 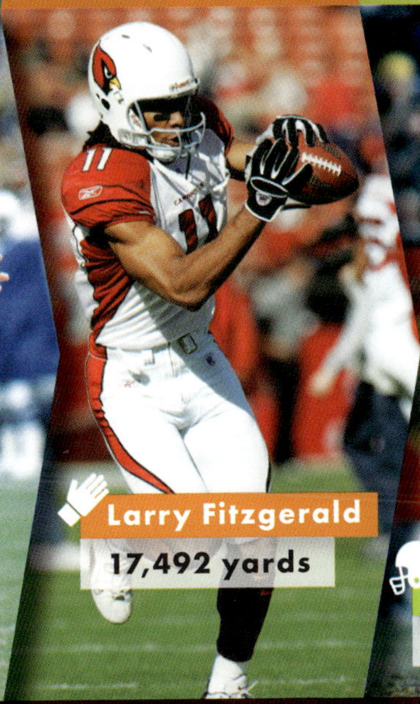
Larry Fitzgerald
17,492 yards

**All-Time Interceptions Leader** 
Larry Wilson
52 interceptions

**All-Time Rushing Leader** 
Ottis Anderson
7,999 yards

# GLOSSARY

**championship**—a contest to decide the best team or person

**division**—a group of NFL teams from the same area that often play against each other; there are eight divisions in the NFL.

**franchise**—an official team of the NFL

**Hail Mary**—a long, usually unsuccessful pass made in the last few seconds of a game

**mascot**—an animal or symbol that represents a sports team

**playoffs**—games played after the regular season is over; playoff games determine which teams play in the championship game.

**quarterback**—a player whose main job is to throw and hand off the ball

**retractable**—able to be drawn back

**rivals**—long-standing opponents

**stadium**—an arena where sports are played

**Super Bowl**—the annual championship game of the NFL

**wide receiver**—a player whose main job is to catch passes from the quarterback

# TO LEARN MORE

### AT THE LIBRARY

Anderson, Josh. *Arizona Cardinals*. Mankato, Minn.: The Child's World, 2022.

Ellenport, Craig. *The Story of the Arizona Cardinals*. Minneapolis, Minn.: Kaleidoscope, 2020.

Omoth, Tyler. *Football Fun*. Mankato, Minn.: Capstone Publishing, 2021.

### ON THE WEB

## FACTSURFER

Factsurfer.com gives you a safe, fun way to find more information.

1. Go to www.factsurfer.com.

2. Enter "Arizona Cardinals" into the search box and click 🔍.

3. Select your book cover to see a list of related content.

# INDEX

Arizona Cardinals facts, 20–21
Big Red Siren, 16
championships, 6
cheer, 18
Chicago, Illinois, 6, 7
colors, 7, 16, 18, 20
famous players, 19
fans, 16, 18
Fitzgerald, Larry, 12
Glendale, Arizona, 14, 15
Hart, Jim, 8
history, 4, 5, 6, 7, 8, 9, 10, 11, 12, 13, 15
Hopkins, DeAndre, 5
mascot, 16, 17, 20
Murray, Kyler, 4, 13

name, 7
National Football League (NFL), 6, 18, 20
NFC West, 15, 20
O'Brien, Chris, 7
Phoenix, Arizona, 9
playoffs, 8, 10, 13
positions, 4, 5, 8, 12, 13
records, 12, 21
rivals, 15
St. Louis, Missouri, 8
State Farm Stadium, 14, 15, 20
Super Bowl, 11
timeline, 21
trophy case, 13

The images in this book are reproduced through the courtesy of: Gregory Trott/ AP Images, cover (hero); DCornelius, cover (stadium), 15; All-Pro Reels/ Wikipedia, p. 3; Norm Hall/ Getty, pp. 4-5; Christian Petersen/ Getty, pp. 5, 15 (2015); Bettmann/ Getty, p. 6; JaySi, pp. 6-7; David Durochik/ AP Images, pp. 8, 19 (Dan Diedorf); George Rose/ Getty, p. 9; Brian Bahr/ Getty, pp. 10, 21 (1999); Zuma Press Inc./ Alamy, pp. 11, 21 (2009); L.G. Patterson/ AP Images, p. 12; Abbie Parr/ Getty, p. 14; NFL/ Wikipedia, pp. 15 (Cardinals logo), 20 (Cardinals logo, Rams logo, 49ers logo, Seahawks logo, NFC logo); Paul Spinelli, p. 16; Jeff Lewis/ AP Images, pp. 16-17; Franklin/ AP Images, pp. 18-19; The Sporting News/ Getty, p. 19 (Charley Trippi); Tony Tomsic/ AP Images p. 19 (Larry Wilson); Michael Hickey/ Getty, p. 19 (Larry Fitzgerald); Larry Maurer/ Getty, p. 19 (Kurt Warner); Rick Scuteri/ AP Images, p. 20 (mascot); Operation 2023/ Alamy, p. 20 (mascot); Fma12/ Wikipedia, p. 21 (1898); MediaNews Group/ Reading Eagle/ Getty, p. 21 (1925); Focus On Sport/ Getty, p. 21 (Jim Hart, Ottis Anderson); Greg Trot/ AP Images, p. 21 (Larry Fitzgerald); Vernon Biever/ AP Images, p. 21 (Larry Wilson); Steve Jacobson, p. 23.